Jon Riccio

Eye, Romanov

SurVision Books

First published in 2021 by
SurVision Books
Dublin, Ireland
Reggio di Calabria, Italy
www.survisionmagazine.com

Copyright © Jon Riccio, 2021

Cover image: *Evolution of the Eyes on a Peacock's Train* by Henrik Grönvold. From *A Monograph of the Pheasants, volume 4* by William Beebe, 1922; in the public domain.

Design © SurVision Books, 2021

ISBN: 978-1-912963-24-9

This book is in copyright. No part of this publication may be reproduced, stored in a retrieval system, or transmitted in any form or by any means without the prior permission in writing from the publisher.

Acknowledgments

Grateful acknowledgment is made to the editors of the following, in which some of these poems, or versions of them, originally appeared:

The Collidescope: "Cures for Acute Macular Neuroretinopathy," "Disease-iversary with Hall & Oates &"

The Ekphrastic Review: "Lipogram Variations" (A, E, I, O, U)

Inverted Syntax: "Visual Field"

Jet Fuel Review: "Clots"

Manzano Mountain Review: "The Finland Poem"

Oxidant|Engine: "We Say Hivemind, Negate the Honey"

Surreal Poetics: "On Literacy with Acute Macular Neuroretinopathy"

White Whale Review: "Five Fragments," "OctoPoetics"

Wordgathering: "It's a Petoskey Stone," "The Contrast Portion of Your MRI"

Thank you to the University of Southern Mississippi's Center for Writers, University of Arizona MFA Program and Poetry Center, Vermont College of Fine Arts Postgraduate Writers' Conference, Ryka Aoki, Angela Ball, Kate Bernheimer, Bob Carr, Adam Clay, Lisa Cole, Eduardo C. Corral, Noah Devros, Patrick Donnelly, Jillian Etheridge, Brandi George, Natalie Griner, Jessica Guzman, Rebecca Haddad, Karlie Herndon, Joe Holt, Ellen Lesser, Sharonne Meyerson, Jia Oak Baker, Judy and Tony Riccio, Nickalus Rupert, John Rybicki, Matthew Schmidt, Adam al-Sirgany, Tricia Schwerdtman, Susan Levi Wallach, Andrea Watson, and Ingrid Wenzler.

In loving memory of Angela Brown.

Contents

Visual Field	5
The Contrast Portion of Your MRI	6
Alexei Romanov	7
Grigori Rasputin	8
Lipogram Variations: Removal of A	9
It's a Petoskey Stone,	10
The Finland Poem	11
On Literacy with Acute Macular Neuroretinopathy	12
Anastasia Romanova	13
Lipogram Variations: Removal of E	14
Clots	16
Eyes, *Flying Nun*, and Dolly Parton Meme	18
Lipogram Variations: Removal of I	20
Yakov Yurovsky, Lead Romanov Executioner	22
Tatiana Romanova	23
OctoPoetics	24
We Say Hivemind, Negate the Honey	26
Disease-iversary with Hall & Oates &	27
Lipogram Variations: Removal of O	28
Anna Anderson, Lead Romanov Impersonator	30
Cures for Acute Macular Neuroretinopathy	31
Five Fragments	32
Lipogram Variations: Removal of U	34
The Perspectival We	35
Alexandra Romanova	36

Visual Field

I transpose letters, the carnival claw's
doldrums as it decides what to negate—

my sentences coin-operated for years.
One doctor thinks dyslexia in the vanity

plate of middle age. I see *copse* and say
corpse. Another orders an MRI to tell me

why *zinnia* is *ninja*, the macula's nasturtium
astray. Sometimes I think *pirate patch*

and mean *eye surgeon*, bookmark over
each line like a hydraulic press. White

space self-anagrams, scaffolds an iris.
The test, a dotted screen fit to a vein.

I make more eye contact since my
diagnosis, decades of backstory

wrapped in peanut brittle. Hold
my demons, dynamite your hand.

The Contrast Portion of Your MRI

A crimewave could enter your needle puncture,
crosshairs drawn on the machine's ceiling.

Given scrubs, shower-cap shoes, not the gown
you expect. Pay before the tunnel turns hospital

terracotta. An hour ago, you assigned "The Petrified
Man," belt abetting teacher pants. The Hungarian

opthoneurologist corrects your pronunciation
of Bartók, sheet music for his *Viola Concerto*

fastened to your refrigerator by ions less
god-like. Radiology rug, you've made

a tuning fork of the head. A mega-magnet
interpolates dye the color of inkjet

jaundice. Cognition blinks, toppled silo's
conveyor threshes gray-matter caress.

Alexei Romanov

Holy man my hemoglobin, an empire
to staunch what bleeds. I'll not rule

the perch of last minutes, won't think
of rubles or Tchaikovsky suites.

Propaganda shows me in coat, saber,
the fabric's brace. I have cousins guarded

from scratches, a monk who prays veins.
My sisters need no monastery brute, his vigils

grime-pious. You could crochet a reliquary
tourniquet, braid the bayonet's aftermath.

Grigori they bludgeon. Peasants too styptic
for miracles re-sovereign the wound.

Grigori Rasputin

Czarevitch stipple-governed, cosmology
sutures what a physician does not.

Nicholas, the treaty dies in a basement.
Odor—because I fear mysticism

bathed away. Augur—I vellum magpies
of belief. Cyanide rankles my beard,

submergence cloisters the lungs.
Benediction coronates you, Alexei.

What empire toxins, folk eyes rebuke.
Your blood my atonement strait.

Lipogram Variations: Removal of A

Ego over dinner with driver of EMT
the hour we went vowel-less,

stocked the comfort foods
of meteor scientists.

Colon-flense this sentence,
                its period too fibrous,
the gurgling pulpit to your gig line, fig-left.

Prynne, New Mexico; Hester, Vermont.

        Olympic-sized testosteroner Phelps
                meets with chlorine pitchmen,
                dungeon for Pistorius.

              Elvis mimic,
        hound dog discomfiting,

              nicotine's compromised positron
      driving prices in the direction of JC Penney.

Periwinkle filed under femme:
    the Indigo Girls' top groupie,
        my nonprofit boss.

It's a Petoskey Stone,

I think of my eye photograph on the surgeon's screen,
macular abnormalities simmering retinal yolk.

Nobody outside Michigan cares about the Petoskey stone,
pebble glorified to passage rite. See one skip one,

peninsular youth complete. Outside Mississippi,
the nearest specialist for my diseased eye

practices in New Orleans. He's booked Mardi Gras
on. Some want the king cake, I want to normally

read. *Chartwork*—sounds nautical—anchor
lodged in sclera. Hematite, your touristy

luster usurped by asparagus stands during
beach season. I promise not to stare at the sun

        on Michigan license plates
bridging my vision changes each week.

The Finland Poem

We teach Sunday school, take the Judeo payola.
A nomad collects fright wigs in the face of slings.

Glossolalia out-saints—
                    the Norwegian
and the air marshal predicating
the syntax of scotch tape.

Wander lithographer,
dust jacket spokestragedy.

Burn litmus, Helsinki of paperclips.
Parabola conscript.

On Literacy with Acute Macular Neuroretinopathy

Creamsicle is crematorium's opposite yet both connote love.
I wear the name necklace you gave me, though witness

relocation says don't. Thesauruses killed imagination
so stop blaming the Weimaraner screensaver.

I'm down with onomatopoeia but synesthesia
gets jealous, adjectives the dueling banjos

of poetry. Grand prize for superannuated
letter: K when you've got Q and C.

Centuries ago, school primers relied
on illustrations of bodily contortions

to teach the alphabet. Shocking,
how anatomy achieved its W.

My friend adores *autodidact*,
syllables down-feathered by Ds,

Ts like the silverware that stirs
a mixed drink. Doctors coined

this disease in 1975. I corrected
neural figure eights last week.

Anastasia Romanova

Father's head shepherding, muskets divine
which duchess dies first. Tarnish tovarish,

meaningless to a mineshaft, exile
gregarious once you pointblank

a king. They catalogue czarinas.
We outjewel a death sentence,

telegraph palace remains. I wish
my impostors proletariat immunity,

a dacha with audience door—
fall opposite a widow's peak.

Lipogram Variations: Removal of E

Strum a grim strip-o-gram
    guitar plus volta.

    Doctor, distill my toxic swain,
Q-tip blood, your hour-long wait.

"Watch for my crumb-flint mastiff,"
I say all animal psychic,
    Passion Sunday, Hallmark's not-so-
            cash cow, post-Ash.

Justify that Madonna primordial:

    not virgin
    not burning
    not lucky star,
    Paula Abdul's glum grain,
    straight up.

This ABBA track lacks Anni's "Mamma
    Mia," plus iambic logic from
  Mar-a-Lago
      long ago,

  Dolph's Drago
  da pugilist-diggity crux.
Carl W: sans Vanity,
      will you do an *Action Jackson II*?

Ms. Curtis, can you talk about Dan Aykroyd?
So many films in which you
and that Canadian co-act.

Scruffy Banbury, my porn alias.
Cousin Mary's, Guy Park.
Bill Murray, do you chasm your ghosts?

Clots

A mannequin gives birth to a jack-in-the-box,
says to the harlequin, "he has your thighs."

The harlequin lathers his mandible,
asks hemophilia how a shadow bleeds.

Her son born with polka dots ajar,
the mannequin sells teeth online,
posts ivories to inboxes.

Platelets tailgate the harlequin's stubble,
venerate a towel that proclaims him
Ashtray Salesman of the Year.

His wares clang like church bells
in suitcases, some the shape of heartthrobs:
idol menthol, Marlboro scrim.

He crowns a tourniquet, dams his chin.

The mannequin sends her son for repairs:
ten hours to a neck, sinew inclined. The boy
crouches, weasel smock and facile smirk.

You'd never know he started as twine.

She retires, ministers to the mouthless.
The harlequin expires. Parliaments twinge.

The kid asks about Pop.

She pauses, breath like formaldehyde
on the morning drive. "Son," she says,

"Your father was filtered, drummed the cigarillo realms.

Yes, once upon a Nicorette, humanity swirled.
Companionship loomed. Lineage bruised.

The things he accomplished with ash."

Eyes, *Flying Nun*, and Dolly Parton Meme

Steel Magnolias has a Piggly Wiggly scene,
Shirley MacLaine's cart embarrassed
after the death-news special
on Reynolds and Fisher aired that
Postcards from the Edge clip where

MacLaine's Dorris Mann stresses
to daughter Suzanne that her dress *twirled*—
she's Debbie putting the verbal dukes
to Meryl's Carrie—emphasis on *-irled*
as if her lungs gargled a beartrap.
Steel Magnolias distinguishes itself

as a dale of Daryl Hannah's left-field
career, she with eighties lock on
replicant, Louisiana hairdresser, and
sea being who mermans Tom Hanks.
My vision surgeon has a filmic clinic,

hi-def TV where I sit pre- and post-dilated
pupils, wait longer than magnolias. That
Home & Garden remodel show could
give an iris's ass about my six-month
checkup. Ten viewings of *Steel* the winter
I re-literacied because eye disease stole

my retinal thunder. That would've been
my forty-first February, circa Sally
Field's age when she played M'Lynn.

Remember her start as convent aviatrix,
radar prolonging the wimple? That year

was a tungsten sty. The sclera claims
itself a simulacrum of Olympia Dukakis
playing to loneliness and thirst, Dolly's
social-media quartet the closest to a four-
picture deal I'll get. Hubris vituperous,
thinking I had the magnolia's lock on sight.

Lipogram Variations: Removal of I

The caravan jeers,
    the applecart adheres.

Chevy objects,
    Yugo selects the solar tea
brewed on my brother's Plymouth roof,
warlock buckled and broomed.

        Haberdasher's gall,
    abbess's cowl,
        don't forget the turtleneck,
the dancehall a chow wagon begets.

      You get two poem uses
out of *mollycoddle* and *defenestrate*.

Share an alley, take your colleague's
overheated car when you look for felon-wear
      on Hardy Street.
              OCD means
  you ordered three cuffs COD.

Status quo near a costumer's bungalow,
    my jewels aft of the bookshelf's VHS.

Have you seen *Three Men and a Baby* melt?
There's an urban legend where a ghost-boy
           pops up halfway through.

                    Trade you
            Ted Danson for Steve Guttenberg,
    Selleck scorned for curmudgeonry
    of O'Donnell when they talked
                    guns, control.

                        Somehow, my grandma's stole
                    sequesters the room of glean.

What people don't know about fur
        trappers would occupy a La-Z-Boy
            whose contours maladjust.

Scotchgard, could you be a cycle less?
Belzer, your *Scarface* scene made me laugh.

Yakov Yurovsky, Lead Romanov Executioner

Lenin I've deadened

        them

    nothing to embalm

no Romanov   hearse

    I am kindermurderer / countryman

        problematic—the queens-to-be

    body armor against ire

Anastasia, Tatiana,   monarchy Maria

    Olga unknown

        I am   familyslaughterer /

    more than alliteration of Ys

Your edict   avails from Cossacks to Tashkent

    Vladimir purvey:

marksmanship   order   flames

Tatiana Romanova

Clergy calls us passion bearers. Execution
made me a saint. Pretenders forget.

The Anastasia claimant undone by bowel
DNA. Jealousy obeys no crypt, a liar's

throne opulent as tooth-melt. Impersonate
a three-week Soviet and blunder like kingdoms

or corsets that *Pravda* remands. Blood fallacy
interchangeable, mitochondrial. Alexei,

your bruise-lake, its bed covered in scepters,
queens the taiga disputes. Bone-willed doubt.

OctoPoetics

We raised the starfish,
sold it to the cancer ward,
split an apricot.

*

Ram willows crumble
in July, still Jesus fails
His horoscope test.

*

Striated lilac,
keep the sanitarium
from decrepitude.

*

Ectopic fetus,
loved you like an isotope
of risk.   Good bye.

*

Alien gravy-
money's tight. When all else fails,
crop circle placemats.

*

Cheap lighter fluid,
the calligrapher's only
vice. Sparkle, flick, font.

*

Fuck with a sea god
turned bonesetter, become his
patella and conch.

*

Cartridge girl thinks, *My
toner, his Kevlar, Ten Most
Wanted, here we come!*

We Say Hivemind, Negate the Honey

I watch *Clash of the Titans* with half my sight.
A yellowjacket colony upends the porch, Michelob

bouts from the couple upstairs, shouts louder
than the vulture thundering my chestnut VHS.

The lead's married to a Real Housewife now,
the one who took a bee planetoid and told

them to venom the flesh. We say hivemind
thinking crowdsource.

My visual field came back: left eye 50/100,
right 67, depth nectar drained.

                When the movie's Kraken
goes from menace to petrified antifreeze, I think

of *Mildred Pierce*, pulling for Veda even though

she is acrimony and hatbox glower,
a grifter Thumbelina with listeria mascara.

Many the hazards by way of
                        or perpetrated on
                                        eyes.

Joan Crawford perplexed to the point of cigarette,
Eve Arden's hindsight, noir lamé.

Disease-iversary with Hall & Oates &

Words, if I haven't seen you in twelve months
there'll be a period of mistaken.
Vaseline, I'll pronounce you *vase line*.
Companion, *champion*.
What are relations but tournament?
It's neurology, not lenses, that marks condolence.
The song barreling out of that $8 card?
"Private Eyes Without a Face."
Billy-John-Daryl, how you play
in a Tucson eatery with croutons
spilt into sunflower seeds.
Bride of scotomas,
a slice of vision loss
to stare at each year.
Meringue replaces the maculae
that have literacy by the balls
of my eyes, paperback
rolled into telescope,
syntax mignoned.

Lipogram Variations: Removal of O

Have that trait where the gray eye
is left, blue eye is right?

That's basic grandeur.

          Riffraff, prism pilaf,
     mendacity's bracket's
the basket-able trend.

     All I'll say is ride the Schwinn mutiny,
pedal serendipity's highfalutin.

Sip a Sprite, press pens
   with Bens Lerner and Vereen.
     Flashbulb in a gutter,
       the anticlimax.

May I change the channel?
It's filth's zenith
(rerun a Cinemax).

Centaurs have their place,
ask fraternities and Mr. Ed.

I'm dating a marsupial whisperer and his ranch,
better than the Sadie Hawkins
where I fell uphill
during the perp walk, pre-queer.

Triage wards shun
urges fragged by respect.

We hardwired the thief,
gave him a yam habit.

Edgewise, the mantle talk;
philanderess unimpressed.

Anna Anderson, Lead Romanov Impersonator

Assassination won't recoup Romanov time,
oligarchy that might've, semantics for the slain.

False Anastasia's story begins with failure
to suicide, ends during an *In Search Of*

episode hosted by Nimoy. That a Vulcan
bestows voiceover on empress bombastics

isn't escape; the *crucify* in *Russophile*
as a playactress epitomizes a pinch.

Enigma none-too-phantasmagoric,
another way we Fabergé charade.

Cures for Acute Macular Neuroretinopathy

the spit of a comic book collector, his dozen X-ray glasses melted into telescope

spackle and corneal tambourine

miniature MRI implanted in socket like cigarette butt to coral reef

lashes grafted from world's oldest optometrist reachable by synesthesia gondola

prayer chain, then iris

brow dye stolen out of moldy revival tent, aka Jesus's Just for Men

blindfold bathed in anther broth preceding lunar eclipse

retina tangoing Lasik if the soap opera was *Cataracts or Glaucoma Jeremiad*

...

see the mountain tram,
crossed skis a love letter's
half-ending

I can't rappel
capillary snow

Five Fragments

licorice, the year
we made a carnival
of his slab

*

the library moon
where homeless astronauts sleep

cratering their cots

*

the hologram's
    monogamy,

bride to a laser

*

elixir's cortex,
banshee's hypothalamus,

medicine chests online

*

fractured embryo's
brevity among thorns—

a gene splicer's paycheck, this

Lipogram Variations: Removal of U

The villa wore Crest White Strips,
pomade reflected a falsehood swing set.

Their glee gel eagle-eyed,
    residents hollowed a ventilator czar
        betrothed to fireside chat.

Wasps eroded, octaves escalated static:
    Mister Firearms crowning
        Miss Americoal Miner,
            friend of the Palm Olive heir.
                Breathe Right, the family millions.

Gee, a barbary librarian staging revolt,
the palimpsest a phlebotomist-enervated gale
(Type O cancelled to inclement kale).

    A-blather, abash,
is it time for the third act of INXS?

The artisan clay-fired a ceramic Sarlaac pit,
    another did the brothel's income tax.

        The Macy's lady asked if I was
            some formalist adrift.

    Redact a letter
        and it topples a psychopomp.
  Anon inertia.
    Better glottals lie ahead.

The Perspectival We

We anticipate the llama's power-animal ascent. Hence calendars of them in human careers.
April an optometrist, alpaca toll collector missing the cut.

Weep for the blindfold tailor's death, o un-monogrammed socket.

Wheatfield bench press, pre-intervention Paul Bunyan's anabolic flaunt.

Wheel to library ladder: watch it, you're raining Kenneth Rexroth.

Weaned from astronomy to corona.

Wield a PhD in molecular displacement but careful of houseflies, though Vincent Price makes a good Montreal uncle.

Oui on the Cthulhu tattoo. Kraken my tomfoolery bicep.

Weave it like a tapestry condolence—my neck stubble, your toes—the Hallmark salesman ordered the fabric vendor after months of witticisms on yarnstormers.com.

Weasel basil, roadkill's spice rack.

Weed and without   errand widow.

Alexandra Romanova

What do I know of regalia, charnel pulp?
Martyrdom ossifies, revolutionaries concuss.

Archivist, relinquish my husband's jawline—
succession hinges on spinecalm. No deification

had we been rescued, loyalists depriving
the speculation that finesses eternity:

Alexei's funerary were we long-lived.
Stateswoman Anastasia, Tatiana empress

Rasputin saw you'd become. Daughters other,
pewter and comport—czar ladles found in

Detroit (curiosity an heiress industry), gilded
carafe between honey and orthodox fork.

More poetry published by SurVision Books

Noelle Kocot. *Humanity*
(New Poetics: USA)
ISBN 978-1-9995903-0-7

Ciaran O'Driscoll. *The Speaking Trees*
(New Poetics: Ireland)
ISBN 978-1-9995903-1-4

Helen Ivory. *Maps of the Abandoned City*
(New Poetics: England)
ISBN 978-1-912963-04-1

Elin O'Hara Slavick. *Cameramouth*
(New Poetics: USA)
ISBN 978-1-9995903-4-5

John W. Sexton. *Inverted Night*
(New Poetics: Ireland)
ISBN 978-1-912963-05-8

Afric McGlinchey. *Invisible Insane*
(New Poetics: Ireland)
ISBN 978-1-9995903-3-8

Anatoly Kudryavitsky. *Stowaway*
(New Poetics: Ireland)
ISBN 978-1-9995903-2-1

Tim Murphy. *The Cacti Do Not Move*
(New Poetics: Ireland)
ISBN 978-1-912963-07-2

Tony Kitt. *The Magic Phlute*
(New Poetics: Ireland)
ISBN 978-1-912963-08-9

Clayre Benzadón. *Liminal Zenith*
(New Poetics: USA)
ISBN 978-1-912963-11-9

Thomas Townsley. *Tangent of Ardency*
(New Poetics: USA)
ISBN 978-1-912963-15-7

Matthew Geden. *Fruit*
(New Poetics: Ireland)
ISBN 978-1-912963-16-4

Marc Vincenz. *Einstein Fledermaus*
(New Poetics: USA)
ISBN 978-1-912963-20-1

George Kalamaras. *That Moment of Wept*
ISBN 978-1-9995903-7-6

Anton Yakovlev. *Chronos Dines Alone*
(Winner of James Tate Poetry Prize 2018)
ISBN 978-1-912963-01-0

Bob Lucky. *Conversation Starters in a Language No One Speaks*
(Winner of James Tate Poetry Prize 2018)
ISBN 978-1-912963-00-3

Christopher Prewitt. *Paradise Hammer*
(Winner of James Tate Poetry Prize 2018)
ISBN 978-1-9995903-9-0

Mikko Harvey & Jake Bauer. *Idaho Falls*
(Winner of James Tate Poetry Prize 2018)
ISBN 978-1-912963-02-7

Tony Bailie. *Mountain Under Heaven*
(Winner of James Tate Poetry Prize 2019)
ISBN 978-1-912963-09-6

Nicholas Alexander Hayes. *Amorphous Organics*
(Winner of James Tate Poetry Prize 2019)
ISBN 978-1-912963-10-2

John Bradley. *Spontaneous Mummification*
(Winner of James Tate Poetry Prize 2019)
ISBN 978-1-912963-13-3

John Thomas Allen. *Rolling in the Third Eye*
(Winner of James Tate Poetry Prize 2019)
ISBN 978-1-912963-15-7

Gary Glauber. *The Covalence of Equanimity*
(Winner of James Tate Poetry Prize 2019)
ISBN 978-1-912963-12-6

Charles Kell. *Pierre Mask*
(Winner of James Tate Poetry Prize 2019)
ISBN 978-1-912963-19-5

Alan Elyshevitz. *Mortal Hours*
(Winner of James Tate Poetry Prize 2020)
ISBN 978-1-912963-21-8

Henry Finch. *Reversing Falls*
(Winner of James Tate Poetry Prize 2020)
ISBN 978-1-912963-22-5

Maria Grazia Calandrone. *Fossils*
Translated from Italian
(New Poetics: Italy)
ISBN 978-1-9995903-6-9

Sergey Biryukov. *Transformations*
Translated from Russian
(New Poetics: Russia)
ISBN 978-1-9995903-5-2

Alexander Korotko. *Irrazionalismo*
Translated from Russian
(New Poetics: Ukraine)
ISBN 978-1-912963-06-5

Anton G. Leitner. *Selected Poems 1981–2015*
Translated from German
ISBN 978-1-9995903-8-3

message-door: An Anthology of Contemporary Surrealist Poetry from Russia (bilingual)
Edited and translated from Russian by Anatoly Kudryavitsky
ISBN 978-1-912963-17-1

Seeds of Gravity: An Anthology of Contemporary Surrealist Poetry from Ireland
Edited by Anatoly Kudryavitsky
ISBN 978-1-912963-18-8

All our books are available to order via
http://survisionmagazine.com/books.htm

www.ingramcontent.com/pod-product-compliance
Lightning Source LLC
Chambersburg PA
CBHW061310040426
42444CB00010B/2585